MW01130335

Presented to

_____

by

_____

on

_____

At David C Cook, we equip the local church around the corner and around the globe to make disciples. Come see how we are working together—go to **www.davidccook.com**. Thank you!

God's Story for Me Bible

104 Life-Shaping Bible Stories for Children

transforming lives together

GOD'S STORY FOR ME BIBLE
Published by David C Cook
4050 Lee Vance Drive
Colorado Springs, CO 80918 U.S.A.

Integrity Music Limited, a Division of David C Cook
Brighton, East Sussex BN1 2RE, England

Library of Congress Control Number 2017950143
ISBN 978-0-8307-7200-1

Illustrated by Cheryl Nobens

Printed in South Korea

4 5 6 7 8 9 10 11 12 13

031220

Dear Parents,

God has a story to tell you and your child. It's the one true love story from which all other love stories flow. *God's Story for Me Bible* is designed to write this never-ending love story forever in the heart and life of your child.

You and your child will enjoy

- reading this storybook at bedtime or family time;

- getting into the action of each story through the colorful illustrations;

- talking about the meaning of each story as you use each story's interactive conversation starter; and

- personalizing the storybook with cool stickers.

So as you look at the pictures, read each story told in words your child will understand, and connect the story to your child's life, you'll be leading your child to faith in Jesus.

God's Story for Me Bible

104 Life-Shaping Bible Stories for Children

New Testament

Old Testament

God Makes the World
Genesis 1:1–19

In the beginning, there were no tall trees. There were no flowers, no animals, and no people! There was only DARKNESS. But God was there. And this is what God did.

First, God said, "Let there be LIGHT!" And just like that, there was light! God called the light day. God also made the quiet dark time. He called it night.

Next, God made the sky—high and blue. God
made fluffy white clouds that floated in the wide
blue sky.

God put some water here and some water there. Rivers and lakes flowed into oceans. God made big mountains and small hills. The land kept the waters apart.

Then God said, "Trees, grass—grow! Fruit and flowers—grow!" And they did! Tall trees, soft green grass, fruit trees, vegetable plants, tiny flowers, and berry bushes all began to grow.

God made the world to show His power and His love for us.

But God was not finished! God made special lights in the sky. God made the sun to shine in the daytime. He made the moon that glows in the night. God made every star that twinkles in the sky.

God Makes Animals

Genesis 1:20–25

God's world was full of mountains and trees. It had oceans and lakes. But it was very still. No fish swam in the water. No birds flew in the sky. It was quiet.

God said, "Let the water be filled with living things!" And then little shiny fish wiggled and scooted. Red and blue and yellow fish swam fast, and sea horses bobbed.

Whales flipped their tails, and dolphins jumped and swam. Then God said, "Let there be birds— birds of all kinds!" Birds of every color swooped and sang.

Big eagles spread their wings, and chickens clucked. Ducks dipped their heads and quacked. But God wasn't finished!

God said, "Let there be animals on the land!" And
horses ran in the fields. Cows mooed and chewed.
Cats meowed and chased squeaky mice. Bears
growled. Lions and tigers roared.

God made a wonderful world and filled it with amazing animals.

Now lively animals were everywhere! God looked at the waters full of fish. He looked at the skies filled with birds. He looked at the land full of animals. God saw that it was very good.

God Makes People

Genesis 1:26–31; 2:7–23; 3:20

God saw the whole world He had made.
He saw the sky, hills, water, and trees. He saw the
sun and moon. God's world was beautiful!

God was glad to see the fish, birds, lizards, and
furry animals He had made. But God was not
finished!

God made a man. God named the man Adam.
God told Adam, "I have a job for you to do.
Please name all the animals."

But God still was not finished! He said, "It isn't good for Adam to be alone. I'll make a person who's perfect for him to love." So God made a woman. Adam named her Eve.

God made people so He could love us and we could love Him.

God loved Adam and Eve. He told them, "Take care of the animals and birds and everything you see in my world."

God's creation was finished! And it was all very good!

God Loves Adam and Eve

Genesis 2:15–17; 3

God put Adam and Eve in a beautiful garden. They were glad to take care of the garden. They loved God, and God loved them.

The garden had many trees in it. But God showed Adam one special tree. God said, "You may eat fruit from ALL the other trees, but DO NOT eat fruit from this special tree."

One day a snake came to the garden. The snake was really Satan, God's enemy. Satan told Eve, "You can eat the fruit from the special tree."

Eve listened to Satan. She looked at the fruit on that tree. She picked it, and she bit into it. She gave some to Adam, and he ate it too.

As soon as Adam and Eve ate that fruit, they knew they had done wrong. They felt sad, so they ran away and hid. God called, "Adam, where are you?"

Adam said, "I was hiding. I was afraid."

Even when we disobey God, He never stops loving us. God sent His Son, Jesus, so we could be forgiven.

Adam and Eve had disobeyed. God told them they must leave the garden. But God never stopped loving them. God gave them a happy promise: someone would come to make things right again.

Noah Obeys God

Genesis 6:5—7:16

God made a beautiful world! But people stopped obeying God. They said mean things. They didn't care if they hurt one another.

God saw this, and it made Him very sad. So God talked to a man named Noah.

God said, "I must send a flood. Rain will fall, and water will cover everything. But your family will be safe. The animals will be safe too. Build a boat, just the way I tell you to build it."

Noah and his family listened and obeyed! They chopped trees and cut wood. They pounded boards and brushed on tar.

They worked hard for a long time. They did
everything God said to do. Finally the big boat was
finished.

Then Noah's family loaded food onto the boat.
They carried bundles and baskets up the ramp.
Now there was food for hungry animals and hungry
people! God said, "Bring the animals into the
boat."

Obeying God helps us stay away from trouble. Obeying shows we love God.

Bears thumped up the ramp, and birds flew through the door. Rabbits hopped, and elephants bumped. At last, every kind of animal was safe in the big boat. Noah, his wife, and his family went aboard too. Then God closed the door.

The Great Flood

Genesis 7:17—9:17

For forty days, it rained and RAINED. The big boat bobbed on the water. Noah's family worked hard feeding the animals.

Would they float forever? No.

One day the rain stopped. There was no more
dripping. Then *BUMP!* The boat landed. Every day
the water went down a little more.

Noah's family waited and waited. Finally
God said, "Come on out!" Noah's family swung
open the big door.

Big bears paused to sniff the air. Hippos, lambs, and lizards ran outside! Birds flew away, higher and higher.

Noah and his family stood in the sun. They prayed and thanked God.

God said, "I will never again cover my
world with water. To remind you of my promise,
LOOK!" Noah's family looked up. They saw
beautiful colors—a rainbow!

God's promises are
for us too.
God keeps His
promises.

Abraham Moves to a New Land

Genesis 12:1–8

God told Abraham, "I want you to move to a new land. I will show you how to get there."

Abraham told his wife, Sarah, "We are going to move."

So the family packed food, clothes, tents, and blankets. They tied bundles and baskets to camels and donkeys. They brought along sheep and goats.

Every day they walked. God told them just where to go. Every night they put up tents, ate, and slept.

They walked and walked.

God is always with us. He helps us everywhere we go.

One day God told Abraham, "This is the place! It will be your new home."

Abraham and his family thanked God. He had led them safely to a new land!

Abraham Shares

Genesis 13

Abraham lived near his nephew, Lot. Each of them had herds of sheep, dozens of donkeys, and lots of goats and cows.

But there was not enough grass and water for SO many animals. Abraham's helpers argued with Lot's helpers!

"This is OUR water!" said one.

"No! This is OURS!" said another.

Abraham told Lot, "Let's not fight. Let's give our animals more room to eat and drink!" Abraham and Lot climbed a hill to see all the land.

Abraham said, "Lot, you choose. Take whatever land you want." Lot chose the flat, grassy land. He and his animals moved away.

God gives us everything we need. We can be kind and share.

Abraham lived in the hilly land.
There was not as much grass. But
Abraham knew God would take care of him
and all his animals!

Isaac Is Born

Genesis 17:15–19; 18:1–15; 21:1–7

Abraham and Sarah were very old. But God promised them a son. Abraham laughed when he heard this news. He thought they were too old to have a baby.

One day three visitors came to see Abraham and
Sarah. One visitor was God! He told Abraham again,
"You will have a son!"

Now Sarah laughed—how could this be? But God
said, "NOTHING is too hard for me! Next year
you will have a son!"

All of God's promises will come true. God never lies.

Just as God promised, Isaac was born!

God Helps Eliezer

Genesis 24

Abraham was very, very old. Now baby Isaac was all grown up! Abraham wanted Isaac to get married. So he asked his helper, Eliezer, "Please, find a wife for Isaac. Go to the town where my relatives live. God will help you."

Eliezer packed his bundles on camels. He wondered, *How can I find the right woman?*

He prayed, "God, please help me find the right wife for Isaac. Have her give me a drink and then water my camels too."

Eliezer came to the town. At the well, a beautiful young lady was getting water. Eliezer asked her for a drink, and she gave him a drink. Then she said, "I'll water your camels too."

Eliezer knew that this was the woman God had chosen! Her name was Rebekah.

She brought him to her house. He asked if Rebekah would marry Isaac. Rebekah said YES!

So Eliezer and Rebekah rode camels back to
where Abraham and Isaac lived.

We can talk to God anytime.
God hears our prayers.

Isaac was glad to meet Rebekah!
He loved her and married her.

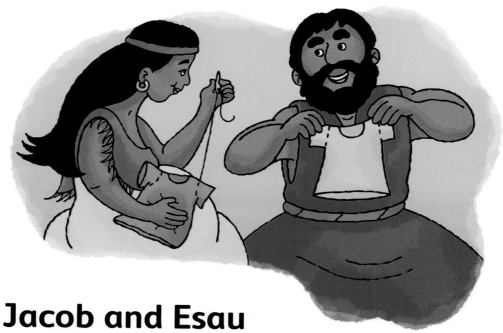

Jacob and Esau

Genesis 25:19–28

Isaac and Rebekah had no children.
So Isaac prayed, and God answered
Isaac's prayer!

Their baby would soon be born.
While they waited, God told Rebekah,
"You'll give birth to two babies." Rebekah
and Isaac would have twins!

The twins were born at last—two boys.

One boy was very red with lots of hair. His parents named him Esau. They named the other boy Jacob.

The boys grew older. They still were very different.
Esau liked to hunt for animals. Isaac loved Esau the
hunter.

Each boy and girl is special and unique. There is no one else just like you!

Jacob liked to be at home and cook good food. Rebekah loved Jacob the helper. Isaac and Rebekah were glad. God had given them TWO sons to love!

An Unfair Trade

Genesis 25:29–34

Esau and Jacob were Isaac's twin sons.
Esau was born first. He had the birthright:
he would become the family's leader. He
would get more of his father's things.

Jacob was younger. He would NOT be the
leader. He would get less from his father.

One day Esau had been out hunting. He came home *very* hungry. He smelled Jacob's good stew. "Give me some stew!" he said.

"You want my stew?" asked Jacob. "Then trade me your birthright for this bowl of stew." Jacob wanted to be the family leader.

God wants us to make good choices and be kind to our families.

"I'll DIE if I don't eat," said Esau. "My birthright won't matter then. So—fine, you can have my birthright. Now give me that stew!"

So Esau traded his important birthright. He traded it for a bowl of stew! The trade was not fair.

Isaac Digs Wells

Genesis 26:12–33

God helped Isaac grow lots of food. Isaac had many animals too. The plants and animals needed water! So Isaac's helpers dug some wells—deep holes that filled with water.

But Isaac's neighbors said, "This water is OURS!"
Isaac did not fight with his neighbors. Instead, he
moved away. So the neighbors got the water.

Isaac's helpers dug new wells. Then the neighbors came to argue. They wanted that water too. So Isaac did not argue. He moved again and dug another well.

There was more water. But would
the neighbors come to argue again?

God told Isaac, "Don't be afraid. I am
with you. I will help you."

Soon the neighbors did visit again! Did they want to argue? No! They said, "God is helping you. We won't take your water. Let's be friends."

So Isaac was glad. He made a big
dinner for the neighbors. Everyone was happy!

Jacob's Tricks
Genesis 27:1–45

Now Isaac was old. He was blind too. He said, "Before I die, I want to give Esau my blessing. He is my older son. He will be our leader when I die."

Remember, Jacob had Esau's birthright. He would be the family leader. But Jacob wanted to get Esau's blessing too. He didn't care about telling the truth!

So Rebekah and Jacob made a plan. They wanted to
trick Isaac. Rebekah put goatskins on Jacob's arms.
The skins made his arms feel hairy. Jacob put on
Esau's coat. Now he smelled and felt like Esau!

Dressed as Esau, Jacob took food to Isaac. Isaac asked, "Are you REALLY Esau? You feel and smell like Esau. But you sound like Jacob!"

Jacob lied to his father. He said, "No, no! I'm Esau!" So Isaac gave Jacob the blessing. Jacob got the blessing meant for Esau.

God wants us to be honest and to tell the truth.

Then Esau came home and learned that Jacob had stolen his blessing. Esau wanted to hurt Jacob!

Jacob was afraid. So he ran far, far from home. He was gone for many years.

Esau Forgives

Genesis 31:13–17;
32:3–21; 33:1–11

Jacob stayed FAR away from Esau for years. But one day God told Jacob, "It's time for you to go home." So Jacob's family, animals, and helpers all began walking home.

When they were close to home, some of Jacob's helpers ran to tell him, "Esau and four hundred men are coming this way!" Jacob was afraid. Was Esau still angry?

Jacob prayed, "Please keep us safe!" Then he thought, *I'll send Esau gifts! Maybe then he won't be angry.*

Jacob sent flocks of goats and sheep and camels and
herds of cows and donkeys—lots of animals! Jacob
walked far ahead, bowing.

God wants us to forgive others. God wants us to get along with our families.

Jacob looked up. Esau was running. Oh no! Was Esau going to hurt him?

No! Esau forgave Jacob. They hugged! Jacob wasn't afraid anymore. The brothers were together again!

God Is with Joseph

Genesis 37, 39

Jacob had twelve sons. But Jacob loved his son
Joseph best. Jacob gave Joseph a beautiful coat.
That coat made his brothers angry!

Later Joseph had two dreams. He told his family, "In the dreams, you bowed to me." This made his brothers very angry!

One day Joseph's brothers took the family's sheep to find new grass. They were gone for a long time! Jacob sent Joseph to find them. Joseph walked and walked and walked. Joseph's brothers saw him coming. They were still angry. They wanted to hurt Joseph!

The brothers took Joseph's coat, and they
threw Joseph into a deep hole. Then they saw
some traders coming. One brother said, "Let's sell
Joseph to them. They will take him far, far away."
So they sold Joseph to the traders.

Even when things are hard or we are hurt, God will never leave us.

Joseph was taken far away to Egypt.
He was sold to be a worker. He did good work!
God helped him.

Then someone told lies about him, and he was put in the king's jail. But Joseph knew God was with him.

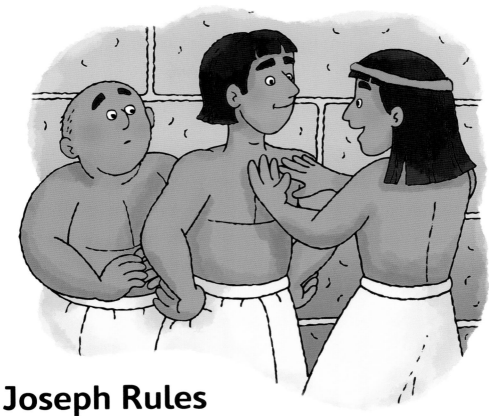

Joseph Rules

Genesis 41:1—42:8; 43:16; 45; 46:5–7; 50:18–21

Joseph hadn't done anything wrong. But someone lied about him, and he was put in jail! Two men in jail had strange dreams. God helped Joseph know what the dreams meant.

One of those men was let out of jail. He went back to work for the king of Egypt. Then the king had a strange dream. The man Joseph had helped in jail told the king about Joseph. The king said, "Bring Joseph to me!"

Joseph went to listen to the king. The king told Joseph his strange dream.

Then Joseph said, "God has helped me know this. In seven years, food will not grow. Save extra grain now. We can eat the grain we save during this time when no food grows."

The king of Egypt said, "God did help you! You'll be in charge of saving grain!"

So Joseph became a ruler in Egypt. His helpers built big barns, and extra grain was put into the barns. For seven years, they saved grain. When NO grain grew, Egypt had food!

Joseph's own family needed food too. Jacob heard that Egypt had grain. He told his sons, "Go! Buy grain for us."

Ten of Joseph's brothers traveled to Egypt. They bowed low to ask for grain. They didn't know they bowed to Joseph—he looked like a king! Joseph sold them grain, and they left.

But soon they needed more grain! The brothers came back and bowed. This time Joseph said, "Look! It's ME! Joseph!" The brothers were afraid. They had been so mean to Joseph. Would he be mean to them?

God makes good things happen when we obey Him. We can obey in good and bad times.

No! Joseph forgave them! "You meant to hurt me," he said, "but God meant to help! HE put me here! Bring our father Jacob and your families here to live!"

ALL of Joseph's family moved to Egypt. They were together again!

God Protects Moses

Exodus 1:8—2:10

God's people lived in a country where there was a mean king. This mean king made everyone work very hard. Even worse, he wanted to get rid of ALL the boy babies!

One family had a baby named Moses. They
loved Moses. They wanted to keep him safe!

So God gave Moses' mom an idea. She made a special basket that could float. Then she put Moses in the basket.

She carried the basket to the river. She floated it on the water. Moses' big sister, Miriam, stayed to watch Moses.

Soon the mean king's daughter, the princess, came to the river. She saw the basket and opened it. There was a baby boy! Miriam was brave. She asked, "Shall I find someone to take care of this baby?"

The princess said, "Yes!"

God gives us people who care for us, even in scary times.

Miriam ran to get her mom! SHE could take good care of Moses! Moses' family was glad that baby Moses was safe.

God's People Escape

Exodus 3:1—12:38; 13:20—22

Moses grew up. One day God told him, "I have chosen you to be the leader of my people. Lead them to the land I promised to give them."

So Moses went to the mean king. Moses told him what God had said. The mean king said, "NO! No one will leave Egypt!"

So God made sure that the king would change his mind! He sent millions of flies and frogs. Grasshoppers came and ate the plants! Animals and people got sick and died.

The mean king finally changed his mind. He said, "Leave! ALL of you!"

The people bundled up tents and blankets and gathered things they needed. And so God's people escaped from Egypt.

Moses told the people, "God will lead us. He will show us where to go and will take care of us."

In the daytime, God led them with a big white cloud. The cloud made shade in the hot desert. God's people followed the cloud.

God takes care of us. He teaches us the right way to live.

At night, God led them with a tall fire in the sky. God's fire gave them light and warmth. They knew where to go. They knew God was with them.

God's Path through the Sea

Exodus 14:1—15:2

God's people walked and walked! They followed
God's big cloud and fire. They camped beside a big
sea. But far off they saw dust rising. The mean king's
army was coming to take them back to Egypt!

God told Moses, "I will help you. The mean king's army won't get you." God moved His big cloud. God's people were hidden by the cloud!

Then Moses said, "Let's cross the sea. God told me what to do." Moses raised his hand. Strong winds blew until the sea became dry land!

The water piled up high on both sides! The people and animals walked across on dry land! When everyone was safely across, Moses raised his hand again. The waters came together. *CRASH! SPLASH!*

The people sang and thanked God. They danced for joy! God kept His people safe!

God Gives Food and Water

Exodus 15:22–25; 16

God's people had walked for three days. They had not seen any water. They were thirsty! When they finally saw water, they hurried to take a drink. Oh no! The water tasted bad!

So Moses prayed, and God helped. God showed Moses a piece of wood. Moses threw it into the water. Then the water tasted good! So the people drank and splashed!

But now everyone grew hungry, and there was no food! But God promised to help.

We can pray and ask God for what we need. He will help us.

God sent small birds into the camp.
The people could eat the meat! The next
morning, little round things lay all over the ground.
The people asked, "What IS it?"

Moses told them, "God gave you bread. Take all you
need for today!" God gave His people water and food!

God Gives His Law

Exodus 19:1—20:17

God's people walked and walked. They walked to big Mount Sinai and camped near the tall mountain. Moses went UP the mountain! He went to listen to God.

God told Moses, "I have cared for you and helped you. I want these people to be my people. Tell the people to get ready. I am going to give you my laws. Then you'll know the best way to live."

The people got ready. Then God sent lightning and thunder. There was smoke. The earth shook! God had come to give them His laws.

God said, "Love and worship only me. Do not make statues to bow down to. Use my name in good ways."

God loves us. When we obey His rules, we know the best way to live.

"Love and obey your parents. Don't hurt other people. Don't take what is not yours. Say only true words. Be glad for what you have."

God's Ten Commandments are His rules for us to follow.

Exploring the Promised Land

Numbers 13:1—14:38

God's people were close to the new land God had promised them. So Moses chose twelve men. They went to explore the new land.

The new land was beautiful! Good food grew in that land! The twelve men also saw people—very big people! They returned to their camp.

Ten of the men were very scared. They said, "The people are too strong. We're like grasshoppers beside them!"

But Caleb and Joshua said, "Don't be afraid. God is with us! He wants us to go into the land."

No one listened to Caleb and Joshua. But they did listen to the ten men. Soon everyone was afraid and crying! God told Moses, "Because these people do not trust me, they will not go into the Promised Land."

For forty more years, God's people walked around in the desert.

Finally all the people who had not trusted God were gone. But Caleb and Joshua were still alive. God had told them, "Because you trusted me, you'll live in the Promised Land."

Crossing the River

Joshua 3—4

God's people were camped by the Jordan River. Across the river, they could see the land God had promised them!

But the water in the river was deep. It was flowing fast. It was scary! There were no boats and no bridges. And no one could swim across that fast river! How would they get across?

Joshua, their leader, told them, "God will do an amazing thing!" So the people packed up to go.

Joshua told everyone, "Walk behind the ark* of the Lord!" Chosen men carried the ark. When their toes touched the river, God stopped the water! Far upriver, the water stood like a wall!

*The ark was a beautiful golden box. It showed the people that God was with them.

The men who held the ark stood in the middle of the riverbed. After everyone walked across, twelve family leaders went back. Each one picked up a big river stone.

Finally they were all safe and in their land! Then God told Joshua, "Tell the men carrying the ark to walk out of the Jordan." *WHOOSH!* The water filled the river again!

When we're afraid, God's power can help us. We can tell others about God's power.

The twelve men stacked the stones into a tall pile. These stones would remind them to tell of the amazing things God did!

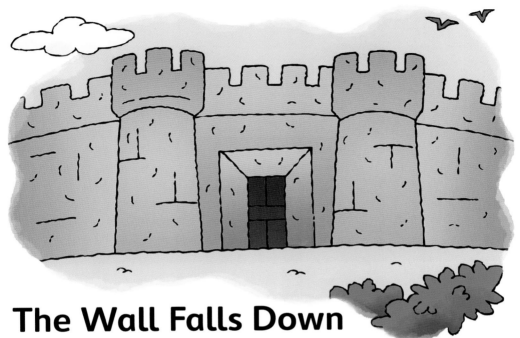

The Wall Falls Down

Joshua 6

God's people were in their new land! But people lived there already. And they did not want to share this land!

Some of these people lived in Jericho. It was a city with a very big wall! But God told His plan to Joshua: "March your army around Jericho. For six days, march one time each day."

"On the seventh day, march around SEVEN times. Have the priests blow the horns. Then they will blow long and loud. Tell the people, 'When you hear that long, loud trumpet sound, SHOUT! The walls of the city will fall down!'"

Joshua told the people God's plan. The big walls looked very strong! But God's people obeyed. On day one, they marched. All around Jericho's tall wall, they marched. No one said a word. Silently they went back to their camp. For five more days, they did this.

But the seventh day came. They marched around
seven times! The priests blew their horns. Then
they blew long and loud. Everyone SHOUTED!

Sometimes God's plans are different from how we would do things. God's plans are good.

The ground began to shake. The wall began to crack! The wall crumbled and CRASHED! And God's people marched straight into the city, just as God had promised!

Deborah Helps God's People

Judges 4:1–16; 5:1, 20–21

God's people were NOT obeying God. And big trouble was on its way: an army was coming to fight them! This army had many strong chariots! So God's people finally asked Him for help.

God told a leader named Deborah, "Tell Barak the
army general that I said, 'Get lots of men. I will
help you defeat that big army.'"

But Barak was afraid! He said, "Deborah, I will go
IF you go with me. If you don't go, I won't go."

Deborah told him, "I will go with you."

Barak asked God's people to help. Soon lots of men came together. They all climbed Mount Tabor. From the mountain, they could see nine hundred chariots rolling across the flat land. The chariots came closer and closer.

Deborah told Barak, "Go! God will help you. You will win!" Barak did what Deborah said, and just like that, God won the battle!

We don't have to be afraid in scary times. We can trust God. He will help us.

When the battle was over, Deborah and Barak sang. They sang about the way God won the battle! Everyone praised God!

God Helps Gideon

Judges 6:1—7:21

God's people were not obeying God. And now they were in trouble. The Midianites were stealing their food! God's people were hiding because of their fear. They finally asked God for His help!

God sent an angel to Gideon. The angel said, "God wants to help you get the Midianites out of Israel."

At first, Gideon was scared. He asked God to show His power by making some fleece wet, and then dry. God did! Then Gideon bravely obeyed God!

Gideon gathered men to be soldiers. But God said there were too many. So Gideon said, "If you are scared, you may go home!" Many men went home!

Then God told Gideon, "There are still too many men." God wanted Gideon to know that GOD would win the battle, not soldiers! So Gideon sent even more men home.

Then God told Gideon just what to do. He gave everyone a trumpet, a jar, and a torch. The men circled the Midianite camp. In the dark, they lit the torches. They covered them with the jars. Then at Gideon's signal, everyone broke the jars, blew the trumpets, and shouted!

God cares for us. He will help us know what to do when people are mean to us.

The Midianites heard the noise.
They saw the lights—and ran! Gideon and
his men chased them away. God saved His people,
just as He promised. God did not need a big army!

Ruth Is Faithful

Ruth 1–4

Ruth and Naomi were alone. They had no food.
They had no money to buy food.

So Ruth and Naomi walked and walked. They came to Bethlehem. It was Naomi's hometown. At that time, the barley was ripe.

Ruth went to a barley field. She walked after the harvest workers and picked up the barley they left.

She took it home to share with Naomi. Now they had food! Ruth was glad to help Naomi.

Someone had noticed Ruth working. His name was
Boaz. He owned the field where Ruth worked. He
saw how kind Ruth was. He gave Ruth extra barley.
He said, "Please, stay in my field. Drink water from
my water jars."

God wants us to care about others and work hard to help them.

Boaz helped Ruth and Naomi. He helped Naomi get her land back. Then Boaz and Ruth got married! Then they had a baby named Obed.* Ruth and Naomi were so happy!

*Obed grew up. His son was Jesse. Then Jesse had a son named David. David bcame Israel's great king!

God Hears Hannah

1 Samuel 1; 2:11, 18–21, 26

Hannah had no children. That made her very sad!

Every year Hannah and her husband worshipped God at the tabernacle. The tabernacle was the big tent where God's people prayed to God.

One day Hannah whispered to God, "Please, give me a son. I'll teach him to love and obey You. Please, give me a baby!"

Eli the teacher saw Hannah. He said, "May God give you what you've asked." Hannah went home very happy! She knew God listens.

Months later, baby Samuel was born! Hannah took
good care of him! Then Samuel grew older. Hannah
took him to the tabernacle.

Samuel lived and worked there with Eli. And every
year Hannah visited him. She always brought
Samuel a new coat. She made it just for him!

God wants us to talk to Him. Talking and listening to God are ways to show we love Him.

Samuel grew and learned. He listened to God and obeyed God!

Samuel Listens to God

1 Samuel 3

One night Samuel was asleep. But he heard something—a voice! The voice called, "Samuel!"

Samuel got up and ran to Eli. "Here I am, Eli! Did you call me?"

Eli said, "I didn't call you, Samuel." So Samuel ran back and got into bed. But he heard that voice again! He ran to Eli again! But Eli said, "I did not call you, Samuel!"

By now, Samuel was wide awake! He heard that voice AGAIN—"Samuel!"

Samuel got right up. He ran to Eli. "Here I am, Eli! Did you call me?" Samuel asked.

Eli said, "If you hear that voice
again, say this: 'Speak, Lord.
I'm listening.'"

"All right!" said Samuel.

God is happy when we obey Him. We can learn how to obey God by listening to His Word.

NOW that voice called his name again! "Samuel! Samuel!"

"Speak, Lord. I'm listening!" he said. Eli was right! God had been calling! Samuel listened carefully. He did his best to remember every word God had said! As he grew up, Samuel listened to God—and obeyed!

God Chooses David

1 Samuel 16:1–13

God told Samuel, "I have decided that King Saul won't be king much longer. One of Jesse's sons will be Israel's king. Go to Jesse's house. Anoint* this new king."

*Anoint means to put oil on a person's head to show that God has chosen him or her.

So Samuel traveled to Jesse's house. Jesse called his sons together. Samuel met the oldest, who was tall and strong. But Samuel shook his head no. He was NOT the one God had chosen.

Samuel met six more sons. But Samuel kept shaking his head no. Samuel asked, "Are there any more?"

Jesse said, "One more son is out taking care of the sheep." Samuel asked to meet him.

No matter how old or young we are, loving God is what's most important.

The youngest son came. His name was David. God told Samuel, "THIS is the one!" God knew David loved Him. So Samuel put oil on David's head. God had chosen David to be Israel's new king!

The Lord Is My Shepherd

Psalm 23

David wrote a song about how God loves us and
cares for us just as a shepherd cares for his sheep.

"God is my shepherd. He gives me everything I need. He gives me good food and water. He shows me the right way to go."

We can sing and thank God for His great love for us.

"Even when I'm scared, I know He is with me and is taking care of me. God fills my life with good things, and I know I'll live forever with Him."

David the Hero

1 Samuel 17

Three of David's big brothers joined King Saul's army. The army was fighting the Philistines. The BIGGEST Philistine was Goliath.

Every day Goliath stood in the valley. He'd yell, "Send someone to FIGHT me! If anyone can knock me down, we Philistines will work for YOU!" But NO one wanted to fight Goliath! Everyone was afraid of him.

Meanwhile, Jesse told David, "Visit your brothers. Tell me if they are well. Pack up the donkeys with grain and cheese and bread to give to them."

David walked and walked. Finally David saw the camp. He gave his brothers the food.

But while David was there, he heard Goliath shout! David asked, "Why doesn't someone fight him?" But everyone was afraid. "I'LL fight him!" David said. "GOD will help me!"

"I don't need armor," said David. He picked up five smooth little rocks. He put one in his slingshot. He said to Goliath, "You have a sword. But I have GOD'S help!" David twirled the rock in his sling. It went around and around very fast.

God helps us do big jobs. He is stronger than anything or anyone!

The rock hit Goliath's head.
Big Goliath fell down. *THUNK!*
God had helped David win the battle!
Everyone said David was a hero!

176

David and Jonathan

1 Samuel 16:15–23; 18:1–4; 19:1–7

King Saul was VERY unhappy. But when David
played his harp, King Saul felt better. So David went
to live at the palace.

Jonathan was King Saul's son. Jonathan and
David became friends.

Jonathan and David promised to ALWAYS be best friends! Jonathan gave David his own coat. He gave David his own bow and arrow.

God gives us friends we can love and be kind to. We can help our friends.

Later King Saul was jealous of David and wanted to hurt him! Jonathan helped David hide. Then Jonathan talked with King Saul so David could come back and be safe. The friends were glad to be together again!

David Is Kind to Saul

1 Samuel 26

King Saul did NOT want David to become king. He wanted to get rid of David. So David ran away and hid with his friends.

But King Saul's army looked for them. One night King Saul and his army were asleep. David and a friend tiptoed to Saul. David's friend wanted to hurt King Saul. But David said, "NO! I won't hurt him!"

David and his friend took Saul's spear. They took the water jug by his head. They carried Saul's things to the top of a hill.

Then David shouted, "King Saul! Where is your water jug? Where is your spear?"

King Saul jumped up. He called back, "Is that you, David?"

Even when others are not kind to us, God will help us be kind to them.

David said, "I could have hurt you! But I did not."

King Saul said, "I was wrong. I won't try to hurt you. May God take care of you."

David Helps Mephibosheth

1 Samuel 20:14–17, 42; 2 Samuel 9

David and Jonathan were best friends. They promised to help each other. They also promised to always take care of each other's family.

Many years later, David was king. Jonathan had died, but David did not forget him—or his promise. He asked Ziba, "Is anyone still alive from Jonathan's family? I want to be kind and help!" Ziba told him about Mephibosheth.

Mephibosheth was one of Jonathan's sons. His feet were hurt. He didn't walk well. David sent servants to tell Mephibosheth that David wanted to see him.

Mephibosheth went to David's palace. David said, "Mephibosheth, don't be afraid. I want you to live here."

God wants us to keep our promises and help people in tough times.

David said, "I want you to eat with me. I will treat you like my own son." So Mephibosheth lived in the palace!

Solomon Becomes King

1 Kings 1:28–31; 3:5–14; 4:29–34; 6:1–14

King David chose his son Solomon to be king. King Solomon asked God to help him be wise. He asked God to help him be a good ruler.

God told Solomon, "You did not ask for money. You did not ask for long life. Since you asked to be a good king instead, I will give you wisdom. You will also be rich and have a long life!"

God made Solomon the wisest man EVER. He also made Solomon the richest king! People visited from all over the world. They wanted to learn from wise Solomon.

If we ask Him, God will give us wisdom so we will know the right things to do.

Solomon built many wonderful buildings.
The best building he built was a temple for God.
God's people went to the temple to praise God. They
prayed and worshipped God there. It was beautiful.
And God was glad!

God Cares for Elijah

1 Kings 16:29–30; 17:1–6

After Solomon was king, other kings ruled. Ahab was a very BAD king in Israel. He did not love and obey God. God sent Elijah the prophet to tell the king God's messages.

God told Elijah, "Go tell King Ahab there will be NO rain until you say so!" So Elijah told Ahab what God said. No rain meant everything would dry up. No food would grow. Everyone would be hungry!

King Ahab got very ANGRY! He wanted to hurt Elijah!

God takes care of us every day. He knows what we need.

So God sent Elijah to hide in a safe place. Elijah lived beside a stream of water. Every day he drank water from this stream. Then God sent birds. They carried bread and meat to Elijah every day.

God Cares for a Widow

1 Kings 17:7–16

One day the stream near Elijah dried up! So God told Elijah to go to a town. He said a woman there would have food. Elijah walked and walked and walked!

At the town, Elijah saw a woman. She was picking up sticks. Elijah asked her for water. "Could you bring bread too?" he asked.

The woman said, "I have only enough flour and oil to make one last bit of bread for my son and me."

Elijah said, "Don't be afraid. Make a little bread for me first. God promised that there will be enough food for all of us!"

We can celebrate and thank God for all the good things He gives us.

So the woman baked bread for Elijah. Then she looked into her flour jar. There was MORE flour! She peeked into her oil pitcher. There was MORE oil! And every day after that there was enough flour and oil.

Elijah and the Prophets of Baal

1 Kings 18:18–39

Elijah told King Ahab, "You have not obeyed God. You have worshipped the false god Baal. Tell the people and Baal's prophets to meet me on Mount Carmel."

On the big day, everyone went to the mountain.
Elijah said to the people, "Let us see who is REALLY
God. Baal's prophets will get a sacrifice ready. So
will I. Then we'll pray. Whoever answers the prayer
by sending fire is the one true God!"

The people said, "This is a good idea!" So Baal's prophets got a sacrifice ready. Then they prayed, shouted, and stomped! They did this all day long. But Baal did not send any fire.

In the evening, Elijah got a sacrifice ready. He had men pour water over it—three times! Then Elijah prayed, "Oh Lord God, please show these people that YOU are the one true God!"

WHOOSH! God's fire came down! It burned up everything!

God is alive and powerful. He loves us. God wants us to love Him.

The people bowed to the ground. They could see that Baal had no power. They shouted, "THE LORD—HE IS GOD! THE LORD—HE IS GOD!"

Elisha and the Oil

2 Kings 4:1–7

A sad woman asked God's prophet Elisha for help. She said, "My husband died. He owed money. If I don't pay back the money, my boys will be sold as slaves!"

Elisha asked, "What do you have?"

"Nothing—except a little oil!" she said.

Elisha told her what to do: "Ask your neighbors for jars. Take the jars into the house. Pour oil into each jar."

The woman did! She and her boys filled jar after jar after jar with oil. The oil did NOT run out! When she asked for another jar, her son said, "There aren't any jars left!" Every jar in the house was full of oil!

Sometimes we have very little. Even then, God will take care of us and help us.

The woman went to tell Elisha. He said, "Now sell the oil. Pay back the money. Then you and your sons can live on the money that is left." God took care of this family in an amazing way!

God Heals Naaman

2 Kings 5:1–15

Naaman was an important army commander. But he had leprosy—painful sores all over his body.

A servant girl in his house told Naaman's wife,
"Elisha can ask God to help Naaman!"

When Elisha heard that Naaman wanted to be made well, he sent a message: "Have Naaman come to me."

So Naaman went to Elisha's house. Elisha's servant told Naaman, "Elisha says to wash in the Jordan River seven times. Then you will be well."

At first, Naaman was angry. Washing in a river sounded like a silly idea! He started to walk away.

But Naaman's servant said, "If you had to pay money or do something hard, you would do it! Why not obey?"

God cares about us when we are hurt or sick. He will never leave us alone.

So Naaman walked to the river. He ducked under the water seven times! Naaman came up, and his sores were gone! Naaman said, "The God of Israel has made me well. He is the one true God!"

Joash Repairs the Temple

2 Kings 12:1–15; 2 Chronicles 24:1–14

God's temple once was beautiful. People went there to pray to God. But after many years, no one went. No one prayed or sang to God in the temple. The temple was broken, dirty, and dusty!

Then seven-year-old Joash became king. He loved
God! Little King Joash grew up. He wanted God's
people to love God. So King Joash planned to make
the temple beautiful once more.

Joash told the temple helpers to say, "Please help us make the temple beautiful. Bring money to the big box." People gave their money. Soon the big money box was full.

Helpers sawed and hammered. They swept.
They made bowls and candlesticks out of gold.
Now the temple was beautiful again!

Josiah Obeys God

2 Chronicles 34:1—35:19, 29–33

Many years later, God's people had again
forgotten how to obey the Lord. Josiah became
their king when he was only eight years old.

Josiah told his workers, "Let's make God's temple clean!" So the workers cleaned and swept. They lifted and dusted—and look! They found a scroll of God's Word!

A servant brought the scroll to Josiah. He listened to the words carefully. Then King Josiah sent out this order: "Come to hear God's words. We must learn how to obey God!"

Reading God's Word and obeying Him makes us glad!

The people came to listen to God's Word.
King Josiah read every word out loud. He said,
"I will obey what I have read." God's people said
they would obey too! They were glad to know
how to obey God. So for days they sang and
worshipped Him!

Nehemiah Rebuilds the Wall

Nehemiah 1–3; 4:1–6; 6:15–16; 12:27, 43

Nehemiah lived in Babylon. He was the king's special helper. But Nehemiah was from Jerusalem. Nehemiah heard that the wall in Jerusalem was broken down. Nehemiah felt very sad about this. So he prayed and prayed.

Then he asked the king of Babylon, "Let me go rebuild Jerusalem's wall." The king said yes!

So Nehemiah traveled to Jerusalem. He saw the broken wall. He saw the burned gates. He met the people living there. Nehemiah said, "Let's all build the wall!"

God wants us to work together. We can share the work and help one another.

Every family went to work. Some families built a gate. Some families put stones into the wall. It took a long time. But one day the work was done! Nehemiah and the people thanked God!

Esther Trusts God

Esther 2–9

Esther was one of God's people. She lived in Persia. Her parents had died. So her cousin Mordecai took care of her.

King Xerxes chose Esther to be his queen. Esther went to live in his palace! King Xerxes gave her clothes and jewels. Esther was beautiful.

But Xerxes had a helper named Haman. Haman
wanted to kill all of God's people! He tricked the king
into making a law that God's people could be killed.

When Esther heard about the law, she said, "I will
ask the king to stop this law."

But anyone who went to Xerxes without being asked could be killed—even Esther! So Esther, Mordecai, and all of God's people prayed. Then Esther went to King Xerxes' room. King Xerxes invited her in. God answered the prayers. Esther was safe.

Later Esther told King Xerxes, "Someone wants to KILL me—and my people too! Please save my life!"

The king asked, "Who would do such a terrible thing?"

Esther said, "The man is Haman!"

So King Xerxes had Haman taken away. Then King Xerxes made a new law. God's people were saved!

God wants us to be brave and do good things.

Jeremiah Tells God's Words

Jeremiah 36

God's prophet Jeremiah told the people God's
words. Jeremiah would say God's words out
loud. His helper Baruch wrote the words on
a scroll.

Baruch took the scroll to the temple. He read
the words in a loud voice. Everyone could hear
God's words. They knew they had not obeyed God's
words. Some people told the king about the scroll.

"Bring the scroll!" the king said. A servant read the words out loud. Each time the king listened to a part, he cut off a piece of the scroll. He threw each piece into a fire!

Whether we obey them or not, God's words will last forever. God wants us to obey.

But the king could not stop God's words. God told Jeremiah, "Get Baruch. Write down my words again." Jeremiah and Baruch wrote all of God's words again on a new scroll!

The people STILL did not obey God. But Baruch and Jeremiah obeyed.

Daniel Obeys God

Daniel 1

The king of Babylon marched to Jerusalem. He burned the city and broke the walls. He took many people back to Babylon.

Daniel and his three friends had to go to Babylon. The king's helper said, "You will learn to work for the king. You'll eat food only from the king's table."

But God's people were not supposed to eat those foods. Daniel and his friends wanted to obey God.

So Daniel asked the helper, "Please, try this test: for ten days, give us vegetables and water. Then see how we are." For ten days, they ate only vegetables. They drank only water.

Learning about God helps us make right choices, even when it's hard.

After ten days, the king's helper looked at them. Daniel and his friends looked strong! So the helper let them eat the same food they had been eating during the ten days.

The Fiery Furnace

Daniel 3

Daniel's three friends worked for the king. This king made a BIG golden statue. He also made a new rule: "When the music plays, bow and pray to this statue. If you do not, you will be thrown into a furnace and burned up!"

Soon the music began to play. People bowed and prayed to the statue. But Daniel's friends did not bow. They would pray only to God!

When the king heard about the three friends, he said, "If you don't bow, you'll be thrown into the furnace. Who'll help you then?"

The friends said, "Oh King, our God can save us. But even if He does not, we won't bow!"

NOW the king was VERY angry! He had the furnace heated even more. Soldiers tied up the three friends. Then the soldiers threw the three men into the hot furnace!

The king stood up. "LOOK!" he said. "Didn't we throw in three people? Now there are four! And they are not tied up!"

God had sent an angel into that furnace. The friends were safe! The king shouted for the friends to come out—and they did! The three friends were not burned at ALL.

Every day we can pray to the one true God.

The king praised the one true God.
He said, "No one may say anything bad
about the God of these friends. Only the one
true God could help people in this way!"

Writing on the Wall
Daniel 5

King Belshazzar was king of Babylon. He did not love God, but he did love parties! At one big party, he and his friends drank from gold cups made for God's temple. The king disobeyed God.

Suddenly a big HAND appeared! The hand wrote words on the wall! Everyone grew very quiet. And King Belshazzar grew very AFRAID!

The hand disappeared. But the words stayed on the wall. No one knew what the words meant. The king was even more afraid! The queen told the king, "Daniel will know what the words mean. Call him!"

God knows all about us. He loves us and will help us obey.

Daniel came. He DID know. The words meant that God knew Belshazzar had disobeyed Him. His time as king was over. Another king would take his place.

It happened just as Daniel said it would. Another king took over that very night! Daniel became a helper of the new king.

The Lions' Den

Daniel 6

Daniel was a leader in Babylon. He did the best work
of anyone! The other leaders didn't like this. They
wanted to get rid of Daniel!

Everyone knew Daniel loved God. Three times a day, he went home to pray. So the other leaders made a new law. They got the king to agree: "You must pray to the KING, or else you'll be thrown to the LIONS!"

But Daniel went home just as he always did. He knelt and prayed to God.

The other leaders soon told the king, "Daniel is praying to God, as always! He must be thrown into the lions' den!" The king was very upset. He knew he had been tricked. But he could not change the law.

So Daniel was put into the lions' den. All night, the king worried. In the morning, the king was up very early.

God is so powerful. He will always care for us.

"DANIEL!" he cried. "Did your God save you?"

Daniel said, "My God sent an angel. He shut those lions' mouths."

The king told everyone, "The one true God kept Daniel safe!"

Jonah and the Big Fish

Jonah 1–3

Jonah told people messages from God. One day God told him, "Go to Nineveh. Tell those people to stop doing wrong." But Jonah did NOT like those people! So he got on a ship going away from Nineveh.

Down in the big ship, Jonah went to sleep. That's when God sent a storm. The sailors were afraid. They shook Jonah awake. "PLEASE PRAY!" they begged him.

Jonah knew God had sent the storm. So he said, "Throw me off the ship. Then the storm will stop." So they threw him overboard! *SPLASH!* Jonah sank deep into the water. And just like that, the storm stopped.

Suddenly a HUGE fish swam by Jonah. It opened its mouth wide and *GULP!* Jonah was in the big fish's belly! He asked God to forgive him. Jonah prayed and waited.

After three days, the fish coughed out Jonah onto the sand.

When we do wrong, we can ask God to forgive us. And He will. He will never stop loving us.

God told Jonah again, "Tell the people in Nineveh what I say." Jonah obeyed this time! He talked, and the people listened. They asked God to forgive them. And God did.

New Testament

John Is Born

Luke 1:5–25, 57–80

Long ago, God promised to send a Savior. God sent angels to tell the good news. God's promise would soon come true!

First, God sent an angel to Zechariah. He and his wife, Elizabeth, had no children. The angel said, "You will have a son! He will help people get ready for Jesus."

Zechariah didn't believe the angel. So the angel said, "You will be silent until the day my words come true." Zechariah was amazed. The angel was right. He could NOT talk! Zechariah went home. Soon Elizabeth was expecting a baby!

All the time, in the day and in the night, God will keep His promises to you.

Then Elizabeth's baby was born. His parents named him John. Suddenly Zechariah could talk again. Zechariah told of the wonderful things God was going to do when baby John grew up. He thanked God for keeping His promises!

Mary Hears Good News

Matthew 1:18–21; Luke 1:26–56

God sent an angel to tell Mary good news! The angel
surprised her. The angel said, "Don't be afraid, Mary!
God has important news for you. You will have a baby
Name Him Jesus. He is the Savior God promised to
send—God's own Son."

Mary wanted to tell her good news! She went to see her cousin, Elizabeth. Elizabeth would soon have a baby too! Elizabeth also knew Mary's baby would be the Savior God promised to send. Elizabeth and Mary praised God together!

God sent an angel to another person. Joseph was going to be Mary's husband. In a dream, an angel talked to him.

Jesus is the most special baby ever born. He is God's Son.

The angel said, "Don't be afraid to get married to Mary. The baby is the Savior God promised to send. Name the baby Jesus." Joseph believed God's promise was about to come true!

Jesus Is Born

Luke 2:1–7

Mary's baby would be born soon. Joseph told Mary, "We must go to Bethlehem, my hometown. We must write our names in the king's tax book."

Mary and Joseph packed their things. Mary and Joseph walked and walked down the road to Bethlehem. At night, they stopped and slept. When morning came, they walked again.

Mary and Joseph finally got to Bethlehem. The city was FULL of people. Joseph and Mary needed a place to sleep. Joseph knocked on the door of an inn. But there was no room. It was full.

The innkeeper said, "Wait! You can use the stable!" Sheep, cows, and donkeys slept there. But Joseph and Mary were glad for a place to rest!

Not long after, in the stable, Jesus was born. Mary wrapped Him up safe and warm.

God wants everyone to know about His love. So He sent Jesus to be born.

She laid baby Jesus down in the manger. He slept where the animals ate. God's Son, Jesus, was born!

Shepherds and Angels

Luke 2:8–20

It was a quiet night. Stars twinkled high in the sky.
Sheep and lambs lay asleep. Sleepy shepherds sat by
their fire.

Suddenly it was as bright as daytime! The shepherds looked up. An angel! The angel said, "Don't be afraid! I have GOOD NEWS to tell everyone. In Bethlehem, JESUS, the Savior, is born! You'll find Him lying in a manger."

Then the whole sky turned bright. It was filled with angels! The angels praised God and said, "Glory to God in the highest!"

Then the angels were gone. It was very quiet and dark again. The shepherds looked at one another. They said, "Let's go to Bethlehem and see this baby!" They hurried down the road!

The shepherds came to a stable. They could see a newborn baby inside. He was lying in a manger. They tiptoed in to see. There was Jesus, just as the angel had said! They were so happy! They praised and thanked God.

Jesus brings good news to you and me. God loves us.

When the shepherds left the stable, they told everyone they saw, "Listen! We have good news! Jesus is born!"

Wise Men Worship Jesus

Matthew 2:1–15

Jesus was born! God placed a bright new star in the sky. Far away, some wise men saw the star. They knew a great new King was born! They said, "Let's find this King. We'll take gifts to Him!" So they loaded camels and began the trip.

They rode for days and days. One day they reached Jerusalem. They went to King Herod's palace. They asked, "Where is the new King? We want to worship Him!"

King Herod wanted to be the ONLY king! Herod found out what God's Word said. It told where Jesus would be born. Herod told the wise men, "Go to Bethlehem. When you find the child, tell me so I can worship Him too." But Herod really wanted to KILL Jesus!

The wise men followed the star to Bethlehem. The star stopped over the place where Jesus was! The wise men got off their camels. They went inside and bowed low. They gladly gave their gifts. Here was Jesus, the King they had followed the star to find!

The wise men may have gone back and told King Herod where Jesus was. But in a dream, God told them NOT to go back. They went home on a different road.

Then an angel told Joseph in a dream, "Get up! Take Mary and Jesus to Egypt. King Herod wants to hurt Jesus."

We can worship Jesus too. We can give gifts of love and praise to Jesus.

Mary and Joseph picked up Jesus. They traveled quietly and quickly. After many days, they were in Egypt! God kept Joseph and Mary and Jesus safe!

Jesus at the Temple

Luke 2:41–52

Baby Jesus grew and grew! He grew taller and stronger and wiser. Joseph was a carpenter. He made things out of wood. He taught Jesus how to make things too.

294

When Jesus was twelve years old, His family traveled to Jerusalem. It was a holiday! They went to the temple to worship. They sang and prayed to God. They visited with relatives and friends.

After a week, they started walking home.
Everyone was busy talking and walking. They
walked all day. No one noticed that Jesus wasn't
there!

But when everyone stopped to sleep, Mary and Joseph looked for Jesus. They could not find Him anywhere! WHERE could Jesus be?

Mary and Joseph hurried back to Jerusalem. They looked EVERYWHERE for Jesus. They looked all over the city for three days! Then they went to search the temple. They stopped, amazed! THERE was Jesus!

You are growing taller and stronger and wiser. God takes care of you as you grow.

Jesus was talking to the temple leaders! He wasn't afraid or sad. He was there to talk about God, His Father. He knew God was taking care of Him!

John the Baptist

Matthew 3:1–17; Luke 3:1–22

John was Jesus's cousin. John lived
alone in the desert. He wore rough and simple
clothes, and he ate the food he found in the desert.

God had given John a special job. John told the people, "Get ready! God will soon send the Savior!"

John talked near the Jordan River. People came from all the towns to listen!

John told people, "Stop doing wrong. Ask God to forgive you. Do what is right!"

The people asked, "What should we do?"

John said, "If you have two coats, give one to a person who has NO coat. If you have food, give some to HUNGRY people."

Some soldiers asked John, "What should WE do?"

John said, "Be honest. Don't take money that isn't yours. Be happy with what you have."

John baptized many people in the river. Being baptized showed that a person wanted God to forgive the wrong things he or she did.

One day Jesus asked John to baptize HIM. John said, "YOU should baptize ME!"

But Jesus said, "No. This is what God wants us to do. And I want to obey God."

So John baptized Jesus. Then God's Spirit, looking like a dove, came down from heaven to Jesus.

God spoke from heaven: "This is my Son. I love Him. I am pleased with Him!"

Jesus Chooses Helpers

Matthew 4:18–22; Luke 5:27–28; 6:12–16; 9:1–6

Jesus walked by the Sea of Galilee. He saw fishermen throwing big fishing nets into the water. Jesus called, "Peter! Andrew! Come, follow me. I'll teach you how to tell people about God." The two men gladly went with Jesus!

Jesus walked down the shore. He saw two other fishermen in a boat. "James and John!" Jesus called. "Come with me!" James and John also went with Jesus. Now Jesus had FOUR helpers!

Later Jesus saw a man named Matthew. Matthew was working, collecting money. "Follow me, Matthew," said Jesus. Matthew got up and went with Jesus. Now Jesus had FIVE friends to help Him!

We can be helpers for Jesus too. We can talk about God's love.

Jesus asked more people to follow Him—six, seven, eight, nine, ten, eleven, twelve helpers! Jesus taught His twelve helpers many things about God's love. Jesus's helpers told other people what they had learned about God's love.

Nicodemus and Jesus

John 3:1–17

Nicodemus was a leader in the big city of Jerusalem. Nicodemus wanted to know about Jesus.

One quiet night, Nicodemus went to see Jesus. He said, "Jesus, we know You came from God. No one else can do what You do!"

Jesus told Nicodemus that he needed to be born
again. Nicodemus didn't understand Jesus's words.
But Jesus explained that Nicodemus had to be born
into God's family.

God loves you! He wants you to believe in Jesus and be part of His family.

"God loves this world very much," Jesus said. "That's why He sent me here. I am God's very own Son. When a person believes in me, that person gets to be part of God's family now and forever!"

The Woman at the Well

John 4:3–42

Jesus and His helpers walked and walked. They walked until it was noon. They were hot, hungry, and tired.

They stopped at a town to rest. Jesus's friends
went to buy food. Jesus sat by the well just outside
the town.

A woman came to get water from the well. Jesus asked her for a drink. She was surprised Jesus would talk to her. Then Jesus surprised her even more! He told her about many things she had done.

She was amazed. Jesus knew all about her! The woman said, "When the Savior comes, He'll talk to us just as You are talking to me."

Jesus told her, "I AM the Savior God promised to send!"

The woman was VERY excited! She ran back into the town, shouting, "Listen! There's a man by the well. I think He's the SAVIOR God promised to send!"

Jesus knows what you are like and what you do. He loves you!

Many people came to meet Jesus for themselves! They listened to His words. They asked Him to tell them more about God's love! They told the woman, "You were right. Jesus IS the Savior God promised to send!"

A Sick Boy Is Made Well

John 4:46–53

A young boy was very, very sick. The boy's father, a king's official, was afraid his son might die. Then he heard this good news: Jesus was not too far away!

The official hurried to where Jesus was. "Please, Jesus!" he said. "Please come to my house and make my son well! He might die!"

Jesus told the father, "You may go. Your son will live!" The official believed what Jesus said. So he turned around and started home!

While the official was still traveling home, his helpers came running to meet him. They were very excited! They said, "Sir! Sir! Your son is ALIVE. And he is WELL now!"

The official asked, "When did my boy get better?" They told him his son got better at the SAME time Jesus said he would live!

The official, his son, and their
family believed in Jesus. He made
a very sick boy well, just by SAYING SO!

Jesus cares about
you when you
are sick. He can
make you well.

Jesus Tells of God's Love

Matthew 6:25–34

Jesus sat on a hillside with His friends. Jesus knew His friends worried about not having food to eat. Sometimes they worried about not having clothes to wear.

Jesus said, "Look at the birds in the sky! They don't worry. They don't tend gardens to grow food. Yet God makes sure they have food. God feeds birds. He will feed YOU too!"

Then Jesus said, "Look at these flowers! They don't make clothes. But what a flower wears is more beautiful than a king's fanciest robe. God gives THEM beautiful clothes. God will give YOU clothes too!"

Jesus will take care of you. He knows what you need every day.

Jesus said, "So don't worry. God knows what you need. God will take care of you!"

Friends Help a Lame Man

Mark 2:1–12

Four men had a friend who couldn't walk. He couldn't stand or run or skip! They knew Jesus could help their friend. The men wanted to take him to Jesus, but how could they get him there?

The men laid their friend down on a mat. Each man picked up a corner. The four men worked together to carry him. They kept walking until they got their friend to where JESUS was!

At the house where Jesus was teaching, there were people EVERYWHERE! The men couldn't even get near the door! How could they get their friend to Jesus?

The house had stairs up to the flat roof! The men carried their friend up the stairs. They broke and pulled and tore to make a big HOLE in the roof! Then the four carefully lowered their friend on his mat, right through the hole!

Jesus watched the four men. He could see that they
knew He could heal their friend! He said to the man
on the mat, "Son, your sins are forgiven. Get up, take
your mat, and go home."

Even when it's hard, we can help our friends.

The man got up. He picked up his mat and walked away! Now all FIVE friends could walk and run and skip back to their homes together. Jesus had made their friend well!

Parable of the Sower

Matthew 13:3–23

Jesus told this story about a farmer who planted seeds. "Some seeds landed on hard dirt," Jesus said. "Birds ate those seeds. This is like people who hear God's Word but then quickly FORGET to obey it."

"Other seeds landed where there was only a little dirt. The seeds grew into baby plants. But the sun dried them out. This is like people who gladly hear God's Word but forget it when trouble comes."

"Other seeds landed in dirt where weeds were growing. The weeds CHOKED these plants. This is like people who start out obeying God's Word. But then they start to worry about all the things they want. They forget about God's care and help."

When we hear God's Word, we can do what it says.

"Some seeds landed on GOOD dirt. They grew into BIG plants! There were a hundred times more big plants than the number of seeds that were planted! This is like people who hear and obey God's Word."

Jesus Stops a Storm

Mark 4:1, 35–41

Jesus had been teaching all day long. Now the sun was going down. Jesus said, "Let's go to the other side." He and His friends got into a boat. They began to sail across the big lake. Jesus lay down in the boat and slept.

Suddenly the wind began to blow hard. The wind made a BIG storm! Waves splashed high and wild and filled the boat with water. The boat was about to SINK!

Jesus's friends shouted at Him, "Jesus, wake up! We're going to DROWN!"

Jesus got up and looked around. He said to the roaring wind and waves, "Quiet! Be still!"

The wind died down. The waves were gone, and the lake was calm!

Jesus looked at His friends. "Why are you so afraid?" He asked. "Don't you know you can trust me?"

Jesus is powerful.
He will take
care of us.

Jesus's friends were AMAZED! They looked at
one another. They said, "Even the wind and
waves obey Jesus!"

Jairus's Daughter

Mark 5:21–43

A man named Jairus had a little girl. She was very sick, so sick she might die! Jairus found Jesus and knelt down. He said, "My little daughter is dying. Please come and put your hands on her so she will be made well and live!"

As Jesus went with Jairus to his house, some men stopped them. They said, "Jairus, don't bother Jesus. Your daughter is dead."

Jesus looked at Jairus. "Don't be afraid," He said. "Just believe."

Jesus and His friends went into the house. People were crying because the girl had died. Jesus said, "What is all this noise? The little girl is asleep."

The people at the house laughed at Jesus.

Nothing is too hard for Jesus. He cares for you in good and bad times.

But Jesus went to the little girl's room and stood by her bed. He took her by the hand and said, "Little girl, get up!"

And she did! She got out of bed! She was alive again! Her parents were happy and amazed. Jesus made a dead girl LIVE!

Jesus Feeds Five Thousand

Mark 6:30–44; John 6:1–13

A big crowd of people listened to Jesus talk about
God. They listened all day, and they got very
HUNGRY!

Jesus's friends said, "Let's send these hungry people home. They need to eat."

Jesus asked, "Why don't YOU give them food?"

His friends said, "That would take lots of money!"

Jesus's friend Andrew brought a little boy to Jesus. He said, "Jesus, this little boy has five little loaves of bread. He has two little fish. How can such a little lunch feed so MANY hungry people?"

The little boy gave Jesus his lunch. Jesus smiled and said, "Thank you!"

Then Jesus said, "Have everyone sit on the grass." He thanked God for the little lunch. Jesus gave pieces of bread and fish to His friends.

Jesus loves us so much. He helps us have the things we need.

Jesus's friends gave food to each girl, boy, woman, and man! All the food did NOT get eaten! There was plenty for everyone.

Jesus told His friends to gather the leftovers. They collected twelve baskets of food! Jesus had made enough food—and MORE!

Jesus Heals a Blind Man

John 9:1–11, 35–38

Jesus and His friends saw a man who could not see. He could not work or play. Jesus's friends asked, "Jesus, why is this man blind? Did he do something wrong?"

Jesus said, "No. God is about to do something wonderful in his life."

Then Jesus spit on the ground. He made some mud from the dirt. He put the mud on the man's eyes!

Jesus said to the man, "Go. Walk to the pool of water called Siloam. Wash away the mud." So the man went, feeling his way along.

He got to the pool. He washed off the mud. Do you know what happened? He could SEE!

Everyone who saw the man was AMAZED! "You look like the man who was blind, the man who used to sit right here!" they said.

"Yes!" he said. "I'm the same man! Jesus made my eyes to SEE!"

Jesus loves us. He wants to help us in wonderful ways.

Later Jesus found the man. Jesus asked, "Do you believe in me?"

The man knew Jesus's voice. Here was the one who had made his eyes to see! The man said, "Lord, I BELIEVE!"

The Greatest of All

Mark 9:33–37; Luke 9:46–48

Jesus's friends were walking along, arguing. They argued about who was important. They argued about who was GREATEST.

When they came indoors, Jesus asked, "What were you arguing about on the road?" No one wanted to tell Jesus. But Jesus KNEW what they had been saying.

Jesus called His friends to come and sit with Him. "Do you want God to think you're important?" Jesus asked. "Then treat everyone else as if they are MORE important than you are!"

When we are kind and helpful, God thinks we are the best!

He pulled a little child close to Him. Jesus said, "When you are kind to a child, it is the same as being kind to me. When you welcome a child, it is the same as being glad to see me."

The Forgiving King

Matthew 18:21–35

This is a story Jesus told: a king's helper owed money to the king. The king said, "Pay me what you owe!" But the helper did NOT have money to pay! So he begged the king to wait. The king was kind and said, "I forgive you. You don't have to pay back any money!"

The helper was very glad to be forgiven! But on his way home, he saw a friend. This friend owed him a little money. He grabbed the friend and said, "Pay me now!"

The friend said, "Please wait! I will pay!" But the king's helper put his friend in jail!

When others are mean to us, we are sad. God will help us be kind and forgive.

The king heard about his mean helper. He called the helper in and said, "I forgave you a LOT of money. You should have been kind to your friend just as I was kind to you!" So the king put the helper in jail because he did not show kindness and forgive.

The Good Samaritan

Luke 10:25–37

A man was walking a long way. While he walked, some men grabbed him, hurt him, and took all his money. The man lay hurting on the ground. He couldn't even get up!

But soon an important leader walked by. The hurt
man lay there, waiting for help. But the leader DID
NOT help! He hurried away!

The hurt man groaned. He hurt all over! But now
ANOTHER man came near. He stopped and looked
at the hurt man. The hurt man lay there, waiting for
help. But the second man hurried away too!

The hurt man could only lie on the ground. But then he heard a *clippety-clop* sound. A donkey stopped. Another man got off. THIS man put medicine on the man's sores. He bandaged the man's cuts.

God loves everyone! He wants us to show His love and be kind to others.

He put the hurt man on the donkey and brought him to a safe place. He paid money to be sure that the hurt man would be taken care of. The man on the donkey SHOWED God's love. He was kind to the hurt man!

Jesus Teaches on Prayer

Luke 11:1–13

Jesus often went away quietly to pray to God, His Father. One day Jesus's friends saw Him praying. They said, "Lord, teach US to pray!"

Jesus said, "When you pray, pray like this: 'Our Father in heaven, we love and respect Your name. We want You to be King over us always. Give us what we need for this day.'"

"'Forgive the wrong things we do. We forgive people who did wrong to us. Please protect us from doing wrong. Help us to do right. Amen.'"

Jesus said, "Ask God for what you need. Be brave. Don't give up. You knock on a door until it opens. So in the same way, keep asking God. Expect Him to answer!"

We can talk to God. He hears us when we pray.

"If your child asked you for bread, would you give your child a rock instead? Of course not! You give good things to your children. And remember, God is YOUR Father. He is the very BEST Father! He loves you and wants to give you what is best!"

The Lost Sheep

Luke 15:3–7

Jesus told a story about a shepherd who took good care of his sheep. This shepherd had one hundred sheep.

One sheep was lost! So the shepherd looked and looked for the lost sheep. He called the sheep's name! He finally found the sheep and brought it home.

The shepherd was so GLAD he had found the sheep. He had a party with his friends. Jesus said that God loves us like a good shepherd. When we become part of God's family, God celebrates!

The Loving Father

Luke 15:11–24

Jesus told a story about a farmer who had two sons. The younger son said, "Father, give me my share of the money from our farm." So his father gave him a lot of money.

The younger son soon left home. He made new friends and had big parties. He spent a lot of money!

But one day his money was all GONE! He did not
have any food! So the son had to get a job. He worked
in a muddy pigpen, feeding the pigs. But he was still
very hungry!

He said, "I'm SO hungry, I could eat the pigs' food!
I'm really sorry I left home. Even my father's
servants have plenty to eat! I'm going home. I'll
ask my father to make me his servant!"

The son walked and walked toward home. When he was still far down the road, his father saw him coming. His father ran to him. He was glad to see his son! He hugged and kissed his son!

God is like a loving dad. God never stops loving you!

The father gave his son new clothes. He put a ring on his hand and new shoes on his feet. Then he had a big party to celebrate because his son had come home!

One Man Thanks Jesus

Luke 17:11–19

Ten men stood beside the road. They were sick with leprosy. This meant that they could not be around other people. They couldn't live with their families.

But the ten sick men saw JESUS coming down the road! They knew Jesus made sick people well. So the ten sick men called to Jesus, "Jesus! Master! Please help us!"

Jesus stopped and looked at the men. He said, "Go. Show yourselves to the priests so you can prove you are well."

The men began to run. And as they ran, they
could see that they were not sick anymore. They
were WELL!

Nine men ran and ran, happy to go home to their families! But one of the men STOPPED.

Jesus helps us every day. Remember to thank Him!

He turned around and ran back to Jesus.
He bowed down at Jesus's feet. He thanked Jesus
for making him well!

Jesus Loves Children

Matthew 19:13–15; Mark 10:13–16

Some families were going to see Jesus. The parents wanted Jesus to pray for their children.

The families walked and walked. Parents carried tired little ones. No one wanted to stop! When they saw a crowd of people, they asked, "Is Jesus here?" He was!

The families hurried to where Jesus was! But as they got close to Jesus, Jesus's friends stepped in their way. The men said, "Stop! Don't bother Jesus. He is too busy to see children. Go away!"

The children and parents were sad. Slowly they turned to leave.

But Jesus saw what was happening. Jesus was NOT happy! He said to His friends, "Let the children come to me! Never tell them to go away. God's kingdom belongs to ones like these!"

Jesus loves you. He wants to be your friend.

Then Jesus waved to the children. They ran to Him! He took them in His arms and held them. He prayed for them. Jesus was NOT too busy for the children. He didn't want them to go away! Jesus LOVES children!

A Rich Man's Question

Luke 18:18–27

A rich young man knelt in front of Jesus. He asked, "Good Teacher, what should I do so that I can live forever?"

Jesus said, "Do what God says. Obey Him!"

The young man said, "I have done that since I was just a boy!"

Jesus said, "Then do this: sell everything you have and give all your money to poor people. Then come and follow me." The young man did not want to do that! He sadly walked away.

God is ready to help us obey, even when it's hard.

Jesus told His friends, "People who love money have a hard time loving God."

Jesus's friends asked, "Then who can be saved and have life that lasts forever?"

"No person can do it alone," Jesus said. "But God can do anything! Nothing is too hard for Him."

Jesus Loves Zacchaeus

Luke 19:1–10

Zacchaeus was a tax collector. People did not like him very much. He took more money than was fair. And taking that money made him rich.

Zacchaeus heard that Jesus was coming. He wanted to SEE Jesus! But Zacchaeus was very short. He could never see over all the people in the crowd.

So Zacchaeus ran ahead of the crowd. He climbed
up into a tree! Now he was taller than everyone!

When Jesus walked right under that tree, He stopped. He looked up, right at Zacchaeus! He said, "Zacchaeus, please come down. I must stay at your house today!"

Zacchaeus hurried down the tree. WOW! Jesus was coming to his house! The people in the crowd grumbled, "Zacchaeus is such a bad man. Why is Jesus going with him?"

We can say we're sorry when we do wrong. Jesus will forgive us and help us do right.

Zacchaeus looked at Jesus. He wanted to show he had changed! He said, "Look, Lord! Here and now I give half of what I own to poor people. And if I have cheated anyone, I will pay back FOUR TIMES what I took!"

Jesus said, "Today God's salvation has come to Zacchaeus's house!"

Palm Sunday

Matthew 21:1–11, 15–16

Jesus and His friends were walking. Jesus told two friends, "Go into the village ahead. You'll find a donkey tied there. Untie it and bring it to me." Jesus's friends found the donkey. They led it to Jesus and laid their coats across the donkey's back.

Jesus got on the donkey. He began riding toward
Jerusalem. Many OTHER people were going to
Jerusalem too! These people were glad to see Jesus.
They shouted praises to Jesus!

Some people cut tree branches and laid them on the road. Other people laid their coats on the road. They made the road look like a colorful carpet for Jesus's donkey to walk on! This was the way people welcomed a king!

All around Jesus, people waved branches. They sang and shouted praises to Jesus. It looked like a big parade made just to welcome Jesus into Jerusalem!

Jesus rode the donkey through Jerusalem. At the temple, He got off the donkey. Many children were with Him, singing and shouting their praises to Jesus!

Some of the leaders did not like what the children were singing and shouting. They said, "Do you hear what those children are saying?"

Jesus said, "Yes! God has brought praise from the lips of children!" Jesus was GLAD to hear the children!

The Poor Woman's Gift

Mark 12:41–44

Jesus sat near the doors of the temple. He watched the people walk in. They threw their money offerings into the big offering boxes.

415

Some people threw in lots of money. Their many coins made a loud *clang, clang!* Other people gave only a little money. Their few coins made a *chink, chink!* But they all still had much more money at home.

Then a woman walked in. She brought two small coins. They were worth less than a penny! It was all the money she had. She wanted to show God that she loved Him. So she put her two coins into the offering box. The two tiny coins made a tiny *tink, tink!*

We show love for God when we share what we have with others.

Jesus said to His friends, "Did you see that woman? She gave more than the richest people! They all still had lots of money left at home. But those two little coins were all she had. She gave it ALL to God to show her love!"

Jesus's Last Supper
Matthew 26:17–29; John 13:1–17

Jesus was in Jerusalem with His friends. It was a
special time of year called Passover.* Jesus asked
His friends to make a special meal. Soon Jesus and
His friends came to the meal. Jesus washed the feet
of His friends. "I have done this to teach you to
serve and help one another," Jesus said.

*Passover is a weeklong holiday to remember the time God helped His people escape from slavery
in Egypt.

Then Jesus and His friends ate the special Passover meal together. After the meal, Jesus broke bread into pieces. He gave a piece to each of His friends and said, "This is my body." He did this to show them that His body would soon be broken for them.

Then Jesus passed around a cup of wine. He said, "Drink from it, all of you. This is my blood that shows God's promise to save you." Jesus said these words because He knew He would die soon.

Jesus in Gethsemane

Matthew 26:30–50; John 18:1–9

Jesus and His friends ate their Passover meal. They sang a song together. Then they walked up a hill to a place called Gethsemane. On the hill, Jesus went to pray by himself. He prayed alone for a long time. He asked God, His Father, to do what was best.

A little later, Jesus's friend Judas found Jesus. He greeted Jesus, "Hello, Teacher!" But Judas was not alone. He had brought a crowd of angry men. They had torches and swords and sticks.

Jesus trusted God to do good things, even when people did bad things to Him.

These men took Jesus and led Him away. Jesus's friends were afraid. They wondered, *What will happen to Jesus?*

Jesus Dies and Lives Again

Matthew 26:57–68; 27:11—28:10; John 18:12—20:20

Jesus let angry people take Him away. He listened while they told lies about Him. He let them hurt Him.

Then Jesus let them kill Him on a cross. Jesus's friends were very sad and scared.

Jesus's friends put His body into a tomb. A tomb is like a little cave in a hill. Soldiers rolled a HUGE stone over the door. The men who killed Jesus wanted to make sure that no one could get into His tomb!

But three days later, Mary came to the tomb. That huge stone had been moved! So she looked inside the tomb. There were two angels in the tomb! One angel asked, "Why are you crying?"

Mary said, "I don't know where Jesus is!"

The angel said, "He is not here. He has risen, just as H said!"

Mary turned and left the tomb. Oops! She almost
bumped into someone. "Mary!" a voice said. Mary
knew that voice. It was Jesus's voice! Jesus was
ALIVE! He was standing right there in front of her!

Jesus did not stay dead. He is alive, and He loves us!

Jesus told Mary, "Go and tell the others."

Mary was glad. She ran to tell Jesus's other friends! "Jesus is ALIVE!" she said. "I SAW Him!"

Some of Jesus's friends didn't believe her at first. But they ran to the tomb. It was empty! Soon they saw Jesus too. Then they knew: Jesus is ALIVE!

Thomas Sees Jesus

John 20:19–31

After Jesus was ALIVE again, He came to the room where His friends were. When they saw Jesus, they were very glad!

But Thomas was gone when Jesus came! Thomas's friends told him, "We've seen JESUS. He is not dead. He is ALIVE!"

But Thomas said, "I don't believe you. Unless I touch Him, I won't believe you!"

Eight days later, Jesus came to visit again. This time, Thomas was there! The doors were locked. But that did not stop Jesus. He walked right into the room! Thomas stared. He could SEE that it was Jesus!

We are never alone. Jesus is alive! He is always with us.

Jesus said to Thomas, "LOOK at my hands. TOUCH my side. Then BELIEVE!"

Thomas bowed down at Jesus's feet. "My Lord and God!" he said.

Thomas now knew Jesus was not dead. And the same good news is still true today: JESUS IS ALIVE!

Breakfast on the Beach

John 21:1–17

Jesus was alive again! His friends had seen Him two times now. One evening Peter said, "I'm going fishing." He and his friends went out in a boat at night.

All night long, they threw out their big nets and then pulled the nets back in. But there were NO fish! They did this all night. Still no fish! The sun began to rise. Peter could see someone on the shore. The man called out, "Did you catch any fish?"

"No!" Peter shouted back.

The man said, "Throw out your net on the right side of the boat. You'll find some." The men did. And the nets were filled with fish!

John said to Peter, "It's JESUS!"

Peter jumped out of the boat and swam! He wanted to get to JESUS! Everyone else rowed the boats to shore, dragging the heavy nets full of fish. When they got to the shore, Jesus had fish and bread already cooked for them to eat.

Later Jesus talked to Peter. Before Jesus died, Peter told people that he did not know Jesus. He even said he'd never met Jesus. Peter was very sorry for his words. Jesus wanted Peter to know he was forgiven.

Jesus never stops loving us, even when we do wrong. He will help us obey.

Jesus told Peter about His good plan for Peter. Jesus told him, "Be like a shepherd. Help people learn about me and follow me." He told Peter this three times. Jesus still loved Peter.

The Ascension

Matthew 28:16–20; Acts 1:3–11

Jesus visited His friends for forty more days. Jesus told them, "Wait in Jerusalem." He promised to send the Holy Spirit to help them.

When it was time for Jesus to return to heaven, He walked with His friends to a mountain. On that mountain, Jesus told His friends, "Remember, I am always with you. After I have gone back to heaven, tell people everywhere the good news that I love them. Help them believe in me and obey the things I taught you."

Then Jesus began to rise up into the sky! His friends were surprised! Jesus went UP and UP until He was in a cloud. His friends couldn't see Jesus anymore.

Suddenly two ANGELS were there! The angels said,
"Why are you standing here looking into the sky?
Jesus will come back someday, just as you saw Him
leave!"

Jesus is in heaven with God. One day He will come back to earth.

Jesus's friends were AMAZED and GLAD! Jesus would come back someday!

Pentecost

Acts 1:4–8, 12–14; 2:1–41

Before Jesus went back to heaven, He told His friends to stay in Jerusalem. "Wait for the gift my Father promised you," Jesus said. "He will send the Holy Spirit. The Holy Spirit will give you power to tell people everywhere about me!"

Jesus's friends stayed together in Jerusalem. They prayed and waited. One day they heard a sound like wind blowing. They looked at each other. Little FLAMES were burning over their heads! When they spoke, other languages came out!

Everyone was SO excited that they ran outside! As they ran out, a huge crowd of people came running toward them! So Jesus's friends began telling wonderful things about God! In the crowd were people who spoke many different languages. But the Holy Spirit made the words clear in EVERY language!

Jesus will help us tell others about Him. Then other people can love Jesus too!

Then Jesus's friend Peter stood up. He told about how Jesus lived and died and came back to life so people could join God's family. That day, more and more people loved Jesus! God's family grew bigger and BIGGER.

A Lame Man Walks

Acts 3:1–16

There was a man who could not walk or run. He was born that way. He couldn't work or play or help his friends. Every day he lay on a mat by the temple gate. He asked people for money.

One day Peter and John walked by this man. He asked
for money, as he always did. Peter said, "Look at us."
The man looked up. Peter said, "I do not have money
to give you. But I'll give you what I do have. In the
name of Jesus, WALK!" Peter took the man by the
hand.

The man's legs were made STRONG! He stood!
He could tiptoe and march. He could skip and
jump! He walked and leaped and bounced and
danced into the temple behind Peter and John!

Jesus has the power to make sick people well. We can praise Him!

Everyone knew this man! He had sat by the temple gate for YEARS. Peter told the people how God had healed the man in Jesus's name. He told them all about Jesus while they watched the man show how his legs could leap and walk!

Barnabas Shares

Acts 4:32–37

God's family was glad to share the things they had!
No one said, "This is MINE. You can't have any!"
Instead, people said, "Would you like some? There is
PLENTY for both of us!"

If people needed food, other people gave them the food they needed. If people needed clothes, other people brought them the clothes they needed.

People who owned houses or fields sold them. They brought the money they made to the leaders of God's family. The leaders used it to help EVERYONE.

Sharing with others helps them and is a good way to tell God we love Him.

One man named Barnabas sold his field. He didn't keep his money for himself. He was GLAD to share what he had. In God's family, no one needed anything because everyone shared everything!

Food for Widows

Acts 6:1–7

God's family was growing! But there was a problem. Some women weren't getting enough to eat. They were still hungry! They felt forgotten. Jesus's friends wanted God's family to have more LOVE, not more hunger!

Jesus's friends knew they needed to keep telling people about Jesus. They couldn't solve the food problem themselves. So they asked everyone to choose some helpers. These helpers would work to make sure everyone got enough food.

We all can be helpers in God's family. Helping others shows we love God.

They chose four helpers. But they needed to be sure they had enough! So they chose three more. The problem was solved! The seven men helped EVERYONE in God's family have the food they needed!

Philip and the Ethiopian Leader

Acts 8:26–39

Philip loved God. One day an angel came with a message for Philip. The angel said, "Go and walk on the road that leads toward the town of Gaza."

God had a job for Philip, and he obeyed! Philip began to walk down that road. Soon he heard the sound of horses' hooves. Horses were coming closer! They were pulling a chariot.

Inside the chariot, a man was reading. The man was a leader from a faraway country. He was reading a scroll of God's Word. God told Philip, "Run up to the chariot."

Philip RAN! He got close to the chariot. When Philip saw what the leader was reading, he asked, "Do you understand these words?"

"No! I need someone to help me!" the man said.

The leader invited Philip to sit with him. Philip climbed into the chariot. Together, they read the words on the scroll. The words were about Jesus! So Philip started telling the leader about Jesus!

When we read God's Word, we learn wonderful things to tell about Jesus.

The leader was VERY glad to hear the good news that Jesus loved him! He believed Jesus is God's Son. He joined God's family, right there on the road!

Paul Meets Jesus

Acts 9:1–20; 22:10

Many people were learning about Jesus. They loved Jesus! But a man named Paul* did NOT believe that Jesus is God's Son. He wanted to STOP people who loved Jesus.

*At this time Paul was called Saul, but later he became known as Paul.

Paul was going to the big city of Damascus. He was going there to find people who loved Jesus and put them in jail! When Paul and his friends were almost to Damascus, a bright light shone! Paul fell to the ground. He couldn't SEE!

Then Paul heard a voice. It was Jesus! "Why are you hurting me?" Jesus asked. Hurting Jesus's friends hurt Jesus too!

Paul was surprised! He asked Jesus what to do.

Jesus said, "Go into the city. Wait there."

Paul waited for three days. He didn't eat any food. He prayed and prayed.

God told a man named Ananias to visit Paul. At first, Ananias was afraid. He knew Paul had come to Damascus to hurt Jesus's friends! But God told Ananias it would be all right. So Ananias went and prayed for Paul. Paul's eyes were made well. He could SEE again!

God wants everyone to love Him and be part of His family.

Now Paul LOVED Jesus! He began
telling people that Jesus is God's Son!
He had come to Damascus planning to hurt Jesus's
friends. But now Paul was one of Jesus's friends!

Paul Escapes

Acts 9:20–25

Paul was Jesus's friend! He was telling people in Damascus about Jesus. Some people were NOT glad about this. Paul's words about Jesus made them angry. They said, "We must STOP Paul. We will catch him and kill him!"

These men made a plan. Damascus had a high wall
all around it. The ONLY way out of it was through
the gates. The men agreed, "We will watch the
gates day and night. We'll watch and wait and catch
PAUL!"

But Paul's friends found out about the plan. They said, "We can't let them hurt Paul!" So Paul's friends made a plan to help him. They got a great BIG basket and a very strong, very long rope.

At nighttime, Paul's friends took him to a high
window in the city wall. Paul got into the big basket.
His friends tied the long rope firmly to it. Then they
slid the basket out the window. They let it down
outside the wall!

We can be ready to help our friends. This shows we love God.

It might have been a little bumpy and scary! But Paul knew God was with him. Finally the basket landed with a *THUMP!* Paul was safe!

Peter Helps Dorcas

Acts 9:36–42

Dorcas was a very kind lady. She loved to sew and make clothes for people. She often gave the clothes she made to poor people who needed them. They were glad for the warm coats she made!

One day Dorcas got very sick and died! Dorcas's
friends were SO sad. What could they do? They
heard that Peter was in a town nearby. Two of
Dorcas's friends hurried to get Peter! Peter came
right back with the men.

Peter met Dorcas's sad, crying friends. They
showed him clothes Dorcas had made. Then Peter
asked Dorcas's friends to leave. Peter prayed to
God. Then Peter said, "Dorcas, get up!" Dorcas
opened her eyes. She sat up. And she got up!

Dorcas's friends came back into the room. There was Dorcas—ALIVE! Everyone knew Dorcas had been dead. Dorcas's friends were very glad!

Peter Escapes from Prison

Acts 12:1–17

Peter was put in prison by the king. Peter's friends were afraid he would be killed! What could they do to help him? They could PRAY. So they prayed, day and night!

Peter was chained between two guards. Many more soldiers guarded the prison. But God sent an angel! The angel said, "Get up, Peter, and follow me!" The chains fell off Peter's hands. But both guards stayed asleep!

Peter followed the angel through the prison. Not one guard woke up. The big prison gate swung open by itself. Peter thought he was dreaming! The angel led him a little way and then left. Peter was standing in the street. He was FREE!

Peter said to himself, *God has rescued me!* So he hurried to where his friends were praying. He knocked on the door, and a girl named Rhoda answered. Peter said, "It's me! Peter! I'm out of prison!"

Rhoda was so glad Peter was safe that she forgot to open the door! Instead, she ran to tell everyone, "Peter is here!" They didn't believe her at first. But she kept saying, "No, it's really Peter!"

God takes care of our friends and us in scary times. He never leaves us alone.

Peter waited and waited. Finally the door opened! Peter came inside. He told his friends how God had rescued him! They were GLAD to see Peter. And they were very glad to hear and see what God had done to answer their prayers!

Paul Tells about Jesus

Acts 16:9–15

Paul went MANY places to tell people the good news about Jesus! One night Paul had a dream. In his dream a man said to Paul, "Come to my country and help us!"

In the morning, Paul and his friends agreed: God wanted them to travel to that country and tell the people there about Jesus. So they got on a big ship! The ship sailed for days. They reached the country called Macedonia. They stayed in Philippi, one of its main cities.

Soon Paul and his friends walked outside the city to where the river flowed. People often came there to pray. Paul and his friends saw a group of women who were there praying together.

Paul began to tell these women the good news about Jesus! One lady there was named Lydia. She had her own business selling purple cloth. Lydia heard what Paul said about Jesus. She believed in Jesus and joined God's family!

We can tell other people the good news that Jesus is alive.

Lydia told Paul and his friends, "Please come and stay at my house." So they went to Lydia's home. She kindly gave them food to eat. She gave them a safe place to sleep. That way, Paul and his friends could tell even MORE people about Jesus!

Singing in Jail

Acts 16:16–40

Paul and Silas were in Philippi. They were telling many people about Jesus! They helped a slave girl stop helping her owners teach people about false gods. But this made the girl's owners very ANGRY. They grabbed Paul and Silas and took them to the city officials!

The city officials had Paul and Silas BEATEN. Then they had them put in JAIL. Their feet were locked between blocks of wood. Their bodies hurt all over! But Paul and Silas knew God cared about them.

So Paul and Silas began to pray. They began to sing!
They sang songs of praise and thanks to God.
Everyone in the jail could hear them singing!

At midnight, the ground began to shake! It shook harder and HARDER! The doors to the jail cells popped open! The locks broke! The chains fell off! All the prisoners could run away!

The jailer ran into the jail! He was afraid his prisoners were gone. But Paul called, "Don't worry! We're here!"

The jailer was thankful. He asked, "What must I do to be saved?"

Paul and Silas said, "Believe in the Lord Jesus Christ. You will be saved!"

In every situation, we can be glad and thankful to God for His love.

The jailer believed. He was filled with JOY! Then his whole family believed in Jesus! The jailer took care of Paul's and Silas's sores. His family made a big meal for them. The next day, Paul and Silas went to another city to tell more people about Jesus!

Paul Obeys God

Acts 21:17—22:15

Paul went to Jerusalem. He wanted to tell Jesus's friends there about the MANY people all over who now loved Jesus! Jesus's friends were glad to hear this!

One day Paul went to the temple to pray. Some
people saw Paul there. They were ANGRY that Paul
loved Jesus. They shouted, "There is Paul! He teaches
people to disobey our rules!" They dragged Paul out
of the temple. Soon an angry crowd was around
Paul!

Because of the noise, some soldiers came. They thought Paul had done something wrong! So they put chains on Paul. They asked, "Who is he? What did he do?" The soldiers couldn't understand what the angry crowd was shouting!

We can obey God too! Telling other people about Jesus shows that we love God.

Then Paul asked, "May I talk to these people?" The leader said yes. When the people became quiet, Paul said, "I used to hurt people who loved Jesus. But now I love Jesus too. God has told me to tell EVERYONE the good news that Jesus is God's Son. And I must obey God!"

Paul's Nephew Helps

Acts 23:12–35

Paul was in jail even though he had not done anything wrong. And now forty angry men had agreed: "We will not eat or drink until Paul is DEAD." These forty men made a plan to trick the soldiers. When the soldiers brought Paul out of the jail, the forty men would grab him!

But Paul's nephew heard about the awful plan. So
he went to visit his uncle in jail. He told Paul all
about the plan! Paul sent him to the commander of
the soldiers.

Paul's nephew told the commander about the plan those men made. Their plan was to kill Paul. But the commander had a plan too! He had a plan to keep Paul safe.

God wants us to always be ready to help others in big and little ways.

That night, the commander put Paul on a horse. Around Paul he put seventy soldiers on horses. Around the horses walked four hundred MORE soldiers. The soldiers walked right through the city gate. Paul was safe!

Safe in a Shipwreck

Acts 27

Paul and his friends were on a big ship. They were sailing far across the water to the big city of Rome. It was the stormy time of year!

They sailed on, hoping to escape the storms. But one day the sky filled with dark clouds. Rain poured and strong winds blew the ship! The waves splashed higher and HIGHER. The waves threw the ship UP and DOWN. The water *WHOOSHED* into the ship!

For days the storm kept on blowing! The people on the ship were afraid. They thought they were going to die! But Paul said, "Don't be afraid. God sent an angel to tell me that God will keep us safe. The ship will break up, but we'll be safe on an island!"

The storm kept up for two more WEEKS! Finally the
sailors could tell the ship was getting near land.
Paul gave the people bread and told them to eat.
They needed to be strong and ready.

Then the strong waves CRASHED! The ship began to break apart. The people jumped into the water and grabbed floating pieces of wood.

When we have hard times, we can remember God's love and care. We can tell our friends too!

The people floated to a little island. God kept them safe, just as He promised.

God's Family Grows

Acts 28–Jude 25

On the island of Malta, Paul and his friends told people about Jesus. Later they sailed on another ship to Rome. In Rome Paul told MORE people about Jesus!

As more people joined God's family, they kept
telling other people about Jesus! All these people
needed to know how to LIVE and grow up in God's
family.

So Jesus's friends wrote letters to God's family! When a letter came from one of Jesus's friends, God's family read that letter over and over again.

Paul wrote MANY letters to God's family. He
helped them know more about Jesus. His letters
taught ways to love and obey God. Jesus's
friends—James, Peter, and John—also wrote
letters to God's family.

God has a big family. Everyone who loves His Son, Jesus, is part of God's family.

As the message of God's love spread all around the world, God's family grew and grew!

The Never-Ending Story

Revelation 1, 21–22

John was one of Jesus's closest friends. He told people everywhere about Jesus! To stop John from telling about Jesus, the king put John on an island. But while John was on this island, Jesus showed him AMAZING things that will happen.

Jesus showed John that God will finally bring an end to everything that's bad. No one will ever be sick or sad or tired or old! Jesus showed John what heaven will be like. Everyone will be full of joy and laughter. God's family will sing and praise God.

Jesus also showed John that heaven has gates made of big pearls. The city has streets of pure gold. Heaven has plenty of room for everyone in God's family! And it will last FOREVER.

All the people who love Jesus will be in heaven. We will always live together there with God.

In heaven it will never be night. Trees will grow with fruit all the time. It will be the most amazing place EVER!

Use these fun stickers to personalize your Bible. The stickers can show your favorite story, a story you read on your birthday, a picture that reminds you God loves you, or a story you want to read again and again! Where will you put your stickers?